room 33

P9-CFM-590

PENOBSCOT

DAKOTA

CHEYENNE

WINNEBAGO

IOWA

OTO

MISSOURI

MIAMI

ILLINOIS

POTAWATOMI

IROQUOIS
TRIBES

MASSACHUSET

WAMPANOAG.
NARRAGANSET

PEQUOT

MONTAUK

DELAWARE

SUSQUEHANNA

NANTICOKE

MOSOPELEA

MONETON

POWHATAN

SHAWNEE

CHEROKEE

TUSCARORA

OSAGE

KASKINAMPO

SANTEE

QUAPAW

CHICKASAW

CADDO

CHOCTAW

CREEK

NATCHEZ

TONKAWA

BILOXI

TIMUCUA

CHITIMACHA

BOOK CLUB EDITION

Meet the
North American
Indians

By ELIZABETH PAYNE

Illustrated by JACK DAVIS

Step-Up Books ⌐⌐ Random House
New York

CONTENTS

1
CHRISTOPHER COLUMBUS MEETS THE INDIANS

Christopher Columbus discovered America in 1492. But millions of people were already living all over South and Central America when Columbus arrived. At least one million were living in the part of America now called the United States.

When Columbus' ships first came to American shores, he thought he was in the East Indies. So he called the people he saw Indians.

Who were these people Columbus named Indians? Had Indians always lived in America? Scientists do not think so. Scientists think the first people to enter America came from Siberia to hunt animals. Scientists believe the hunters walked into America. They walked from Siberia into Alaska across land now covered by water.

The hunters found huge animals in Alaska. Some of these early hunters stayed in Alaska to kill animals. Scientists say other hunters trailed animals far down into South America

Scientists think some hunters walked all the way across North America until they came to the Atlantic Ocean. Scientists believe Siberian hunters were the forefathers of the American Indians.

In time, the hunters began to live together in groups we call tribes. By the time Columbus discovered America, there were more than 2,000 different Indian tribes in the United States. These tribes were not all alike. Indians in some tribes had light skin. Indians in other tribes had dark skin. They had come to America at different times. They did not all speak the same language when they came.

Indian languages changed even more when tribes split up. Tribes split up if food was scarce. Parts of tribes moved on to new hunting grounds. The wanderers had to make up new words for the new things they saw. This is why Indian languages slowly changed.

The people slowly changed, too. Tribes settled in many different parts of the country. They learned to eat many kinds of food. They learned new ways of making houses and clothes and boats and tools.

Little by little, Indian tribes began to live very different lives from one another. How they lived depended on where they lived.

2
MEET THE INDIANS WHO SETTLED ON THE NORTHWEST COAST

Mountains come close to the sea on the west coast of North America. Between these mountains and the sea is a narrow strip of land.

Along this strip once lived the only Indians in North America who carved totem poles.

These Indians placed their totem poles on or near their houses.

By the time Columbus discovered America, no Indians remembered their Siberian forefathers. Some Northwest Coast Indians thought their forefathers had once been animals or fish or birds. So they carved animals or fish or birds on their totem poles.

All of the Northwest Coast tribes believed animals were powerful spirits. They believed these spirits gave an Indian the magic power he needed to become a medicine man or the chief of his tribe. These spirits also gave an Indian the power to hunt. Or to fish. Most Indians felt that spirits helped them do everything.

Some Northwest Coast tribes felt the spirits gave them the power to hunt whales. One of these tribes was called the Makah. The Makah lived in what is now the state of Washington. They were great whale hunters. The Makah hunted whales in the harpooners' canoes.

Harpooners were the greatest whale hunters in the tribe. The harpooner always stood in the front of the canoe. Whale hunting was dangerous. A whale might turn the canoe over. It might break the canoe in half with its big tail.

The harpooner always talked to a swimming whale. He promised to entertain the whale in his village if it would let itself be killed. He said he would sing and dance for the whale. He said he would give it pretty feathers.

After the harpooner had promised the whale these things, he raised his harpoon high. He thrust it deep into the whale's side.

The harpooner had a rope tied to his harpoon. He knew the whale would try to get away. And it did. The whale dove. It thrashed. It headed out to sea. The men held on to the harpoon rope with all their might. Then the harpooner talked to the whale again. He asked the whale to pull the canoe toward land. He said his village was waiting to welcome the whale.

Sometimes the whale did turn toward land. And sometimes it did not. But it always grew tired. Then it stopped fighting. The Makah thought this proved the whale was willing to let itself be killed. So the harpooner harpooned the whale until it died.

Then he thanked the dead whale. And back in the village, he kept his promise. He sang and danced for the dead whale for four days.

Then the Makah ate the whale.

3
THE MAKAH AT HOME

The Makah got most of their food from the sea. Makah men fished all spring and summer. They caught many kinds of fish. Makah women made smoking fires to dry out the fish. They had somehow learned that fish dried by smoke would keep a long, long time.

Makah men traded some fish for the furs and shells of other tribes. Makah men liked to wear shells in their noses. Makah women liked to dress up, too. They put shells on their ears and around their necks.

Makah women wore skirts made of tree bark. Makah men wore almost nothing. It was never very cold in Washington. But it rained a lot. So everyone in the family had a bark raincoat and hat. Makah rain hats were pointed at the top. Maybe this was because the heads of the Makah were pointed at the top, too!

The Makah began to shape a baby's head soon after it was born. The baby was tied to a board every day. Then a small board was tied across its forehead. Little by little, the two boards pressed the baby's head into a point at the top. Most of the Indians on the Northwest Coast shaped their heads into points.

The Makah and their neighbors on the Northwest Coast were alike in other ways, too. They all knew how to hunt with bows and arrows. They all knew how to cut down big trees.

Indians cut down trees with stone axes, and with fire. They set the trunk of a tree on fire. Then they burned and chipped at the trunk until the tree fell down. The Makah men used the logs to make canoes. They split other logs into boards to build houses. The men also made bowls and boxes of wood. The women stored dried fish in these boxes.

They cooked in them, too! They could not put boxes on the fire. They knew boxes would burn up.

The women dropped hot stones into boxes filled with water. The stones made the water boil. The women put dried fish in this hot water to make soups. A Makah woman kept her cooking stones by the fire in her house. Many families lived in one house.

Each family had its own part of
the house. Families stored boxes
of dried fish around their beds.

Most Indians on the Northwest
Coast had houses as big as barns.
These Indians always had plenty
to eat. In this way they were rich.
They were much richer than most
of the other Indians who lived in
the United States.

4
MEET THE HOPI INDIANS

The Makah were much richer than the Hopi Indians. The Hopi lived in the Southwest, in what is now the state of Arizona. They lived on desert land, at the foot of stone mountains called mesas. The Hopi were living on this desert when Columbus discovered America.

Like all American Indians, the Hopi believed in many gods. The hard-working Hopi used Kachinas to talk to their gods. Kachinas were Hopi men, all dressed up in strange costumes.

The Hopi believed that a Kachina costume gave magic power to the man who wore it. The Hopi felt a man needed magic power to talk to the gods. Hopi Kachinas talked to the gods by singing and dancing. The Kachinas knew many songs and dances that asked the gods for rain.

The remarkable Hopi had learned to grow corn and beans and squash in the dry desert. But if it did not rain, their plants would not grow. If their plants did not grow, the Hopi might starve.

Hopi farmers depended on their Kachinas to tell the gods how much they needed rain.

The Kachinas danced their rain dances over and over again. Sometimes the gods did not seem to hear the Kachinas. It did not rain for days and days. At other times the gods seemed to hear the Kachinas right away. There were fierce rain storms in the desert.

When it rained hard, water ran down the mesas. The Hopi planted corn in the path the running water always took. Sometimes stones came down the mesa with the water. The Hopi built little dams around their plants to protect them. Big rain storms helped Hopi farmers. But not enough. They had to find other ways to get water to their plants.

The Hopi had found that there were springs of water under the desert. They planted corn over these underground springs. Corn was their most important crop. The Hopi knew roots of thirsty plants would grow down to water. The springs were far apart. They were far from Hopi homes, too. Some were more than ten miles away.

Every day in planting time Hopi fathers and sons ran out to their fields. The boys kicked stones as they ran. The stones rolled across the desert. They looked like the stones that rolled down the mesas when it rained. The boys hoped the gods would see their stones.

The boys hoped their rolling stones would remind the gods that the Hopi wanted and needed more rain soon.

Hopi boys learned farming from their fathers. The boys learned to plant corn in deep holes. And they learned to weed with pointed sticks. Often the boys had to run around the fields. This was the way they scared the crows away.

5
THE HOPI AT HOME

Little Hopi girls did the things their mothers did. Women built the Hopi houses. Many houses they built were four stories high. The women did not put windows or doors in the ground floor of their houses. To get into their houses, the Hopi used ladders. They entered their houses on the second floor.

The women built their houses with stones. They plastered the stones together with mud. They plastered the inside and outside of the houses with mud, too.

The women cooked inside their houses. Once in a while, a Hopi family ate meat. But not often. There were not many animals for the men to kill with their bows and arrows. So most often a family ate something made with corn. Hopi wives knew more than 50 ways to cook corn. Hopi girls helped their mothers grind corn into flour. They mixed this flour with water to make bread dough. They cooked bread on a hot stone. Little girls had to spread the dough on top of the stone. They had to spread it with their hands. It was very hard for a little Hopi girl to make bread without burning her fingers.

Everyone in the family ate out
of the same clay bowl. The women
made these bowls. They made jars
and baskets, too. The men hunted
and farmed and wove cloth for the
family clothes.

The men wove cloth from the cotton they grew. They wove pretty belts, too. The men wore these belts with short skirts. The women wore them with long dresses. Hopi children dressed like their parents. From the time they were ten, they worked like their parents, too.

Hopi children almost never had to be punished. If they were bad, they were talked to. If they were very, very bad, their mothers told them the Scare Kachinas would "get them." Sometimes Hopi men dressed up as Scare Kachinas to frighten bad children. The men wore scary masks with long teeth and popping eyes.

Scare Kachinas never hurt the children. And the children could not have been bad very often. Hopi men dressed up as Scare Kachinas only once a year.

The other Kachinas wore their costumes quite often. They had to ask the gods for rain until Hopi corn was ripe in July. When the ripe corn was picked, the Kachinas' work was done. The Hopi Kachinas could put away their costumes until planting time the next year. Before they put their costumes away, the Kachinas danced their last dance of the year.

6
THE HOPI WAY

The Kachinas danced their last dance in the village square. They danced all day. They gave everyone ears of corn. They gave presents to the excited children. This was the Kachinas' way of saying good-by to the village.

As the sun went down, a Hopi man stood up. He said good-by to the Kachinas for everyone in the village. "May you go your way with happy hearts," he said. Then, one by one, the Kachinas danced slowly out of the square.

The Kachinas went to a special house near the village. They took off their costumes. They put on their everyday clothes. Then they went home to their families.

The next day, everyone spread the ripe corn out in the sun to dry. They spread it out on their roofs. There were lots of roofs in a Hopi village. The Hopi spread corn all over the first-floor roofs. They spread it on the second- and third-floors roofs, too. The drying corn made a Hopi village look as if it were all fixed up for a party. The roofs were covered with ears and ears of blue and black and yellow and red and speckled corn.

While their corn was drying, the Hopi kept a lookout for the Navaho and Apache. These Indians were the Hopi's enemies. They loved Hopi corn. They tried to steal it.

The instant the Hopi saw the Navaho or Apache, they pulled up their house ladders. Then their enemies could not get at them, or their corn.

The Hopi did not like to fight with anyone. As time went on, the Hopi made friends with the Navaho and Apache. Hopi men taught them how to grow corn. Hopi men also taught them how to weave blankets and clothes. In time, some Hopi women married Navaho and Apache men.

The Navaho and Apache never built houses like the Hopi. They built round houses made of brush or wood.

The Navaho and Apache did not stop making war on other tribes. They even had special chiefs to lead them to war.

The Hopi did not need chiefs to rule them or lead them to war.

The Hopi were ruled by their religious beliefs. They called these beliefs the Hopi Way.

It was the Hopi Way to love all people and plants and animals. It was the Hopi Way to be kind to everyone and everything.

If a Hopi was cruel, everyone in the village stopped talking to him. People did not speak to him until he returned to the Hopi Way.

The Hopi were a quiet, peaceful people. They called themselves the Hopitu. And in the Hopi language Hopitu means The Peaceful Ones.

7
MEET THE CREEK INDIANS

The Creek Indians were not a bit like the Hopi. The Creek were not peaceful. They loved to fight.

The Creek lived in the southeast part of the United States. They lived along the rivers and streams in what are now the states of Alabama and Georgia.

Every Creek town had a war chief. When the chief felt like fighting, he painted himself with war paint. He danced a war dance outside his big house. He beat a drum as he danced.

The quick beat of the war chief's drum sent a message through the town. It told the fighting men that their chief had war plans.

Sometimes the chief wanted to fight the Chickasaw or Choctaw in Mississippi. Sometimes he wanted to fight the Cherokee in Tennessee.

The Creek who felt like fighting hurried to the chief's house. They began to dance, too. They made fierce faces. They stabbed the air with their arrows. They showed the chief how they would kill any enemy he wanted to fight. The Creek would fight anyone for no reason at all. The Creek just loved to fight.

The fighters danced wildly until the chief said it was time to leave.

The war chief led his men into the deep woods. They took one of the trails that criss-crossed the Southeast. Indians had marked these trails with gashes on trees.

The war party hurried along the trail. The men carried dried corn. They would not have time to steal food from any tribes they passed. They would not have time to hunt rabbits or deer. Or to fish. Or to pick nuts and strawberries. They had to hurry. The Creek liked to get where they were going before anyone saw them. The Creek liked to surprise the enemy.

The Creek moved near an enemy village just before the sun came up. They lighted torches. They threw their torches onto the enemy's roofs. The houses caught on fire. As people ran out, the Creek shot them with bows and arrows. Then they moved in for the kill. They scalped their enemies. Then the Creek hurried out of the enemy village as fast as they could go.

The Creek hurried because they thought the ghosts of their dead enemies always followed them. The minute the men got home, they went into the war chief's house. They ate no food. They just drank medicine. The Creek believed this medicine drove the ghosts away. After four days, the men thought it was safe to come out. Then they showed off their war trophies. Their war trophies were their enemies' scalps.

8
THE CREEK AT HOME

The fighters took their trophies
to their village square. This was
a great day in a Creek town. The
fighters marched in front of their
peace chief. They showed him
their war trophies.

The war trophies proved to the peace chief how brave the fighters had been. Brave fighters always got war honors.

Some fighters got headdresses of white feathers. Other fighters got the right to wear special war paint. Or to have special marks tattooed on their skin.

Tattoo marks were scratched on a fighter's skin with a fish bone. Then ash from the fire was rubbed into the scratches. Some Creek fighters had tattoo marks all over their bodies. They looked as if they were wearing a tattoo suit.

Every Creek boy longed for the day when he would take his first scalp. A boy tried for his first scalp when he was about 15 years old. Until then, he could not go on war parties with the men. He could not hunt or fish with the men. A boy could not do anything with the men before he had taken his first scalp. Until then, he had to work for his mother.

Creek men planted melons and corn and sweet potatoes for the tribe. Then the women took over the fields. They made their sons weed and hoe the fields with them. They made the boys do all kinds of jobs they did not like to do.

If a boy did not work hard, his mother might hit him with a stick. Or she might dig into his skin with a fish bone until it hurt. She did this to punish her son. And to make him brave.

Creek mothers wanted their sons to grow up to be brave fighters. Fighters were the most important men in a Creek town.

9
THE CREEK CELEBRATE NEW YEAR

The Creek played games just as fiercely as they fought their enemies. The Creek loved to play a game called lacrosse.

Two teams played lacrosse. There were about 60 men on each team. One team was called the Reds. The other was called the Whites. The Whites put white paint all over their faces and chests. The two teams lined up on a big field. An old man threw a deerskin ball up in the air. The ball was filled with deer hair.

Then the old man got out of the way fast. The teams rushed for the ball. Each player had two sticks with little nets on the end. Players tried to catch the ball in one of the nets. They tried to throw the ball between the other team's goal posts. The Creek played fiercely. Arms and legs were broken. Heads were split open. This was just part of the fun to the Creek. When a game was over, everyone laughed at the losers. And the winners did a wild dance around the goal posts.

The Creek always played lacrosse in July when the corn was ripe. This was the beginning of the new year for the Creek. The women put out their cooking fires. They swept the town clean. New fires were started. The ripe corn was cooked. There was a great feast. Everyone danced and played games. Then all the Creek dashed into the river. Creek towns were clean for the new year. The Creek wanted to be clean and pure for the new year, too.

10
MEET THE PENOBSCOT INDIANS

The Penobscot Indians did not have much time to make war. The Penobscot were hunters. They had a hard time finding food.

The Penobscot lived in the northeastern part of the United States. They lived in what is now the state of Maine. In winter, the animals went deep into the cold Maine woods. The Penobscot left their villages to follow the animals. Families loaded up their birchbark canoes. Then each family set out for its own hunting grounds before the rivers turned to ice.

It was cold by the time a family reached its winter camp. And it had usually started to snow. The first thing the men did was to light fires.

Like most Indians, the Penobscot could start a fire by rubbing two sticks together to make a spark. But this took a long time. So the men usually brought fire with them. They carried some fire in a big shell. The shell was closed up in a deerskin bag. Inside the shell there was a burning piece of rotted wood called punk. The punk kept burning for days. With it, the men could start a fire whenever they needed one.

When the fires were burning, the men fixed their birchbark tepees. Their families would live in these tepees all winter. Then the men went off in the snow to hunt. They had on furs and foxskin hats and heavy fur boots. When the snow was deep, the men wore snowshoes. With snowshoes, the men could walk on top of the snow.

If a man was going after deer, he often wore a deerskin over his head and back. Then he could get close to a deer before the deer grew afraid. Penobscot men went far into the woods to hunt. They shot animals with bows and arrows. They caught them in traps.

If they were lucky, Penobscot hunters came home almost every night with some rabbits or a deer or a wolf on their sleds.

The women cooked most of the fresh meat. But they always saved some to dry out and store away. For sometimes the hunters were unlucky. Sometimes the animals seemed to vanish from the woods.

The men came home day after day with no animals on their sleds. Mothers grew afraid. They made the children be very quiet. If animals were near, noise would frighten them away. The family ate dried meat until it was gone. Then the Penobscot boiled their moccasins to try to make soup. Sometimes they were so hungry they even chewed their fur clothes.

But winters were seldom this terrible in the woods. And spring always came. The ice and snow melted. Then the Penobscot left their winter camps. They loaded their birchbark canoes with animal skins and started for home.

11
THE PENOBSCOT AT HOME

The Penobscot villages were along what is now called the Penobscot River. Families were happy to get to their comfortable houses after the long winter hunt. Penobscot houses were called wigwams. They were round, and covered with the bark from trees. Each family had a wigwam of its own.

The Penobscot built log walls all around their wigwam villages. The walls had only one opening. They could quickly close this opening if their enemies, the Iroquois Indians, came near.

Penobscot men were always ready for a good fight. But they fought mostly to protect their villages. They seldom started a war. The men did not have much time to fight. They were too busy finding food.

Penobscot women could grow a few vegetables in little fields outside their villages. But the women could not count on growing much. The ground in Maine is stony. And the growing season is short. To find enough to eat, Penobscot families were always leaving their villages.

Early in spring, families went into the woods near by. They made camp near sugar maple trees.

The women and children cut deep gashes in the maple trees. They let the sap drip into bark boxes. They cooked the sap until it turned into syrup. The Penobscot liked to drink maple syrup mixed with water.

The men and boys went off to hunt. Penobscot boys began to hunt when they were about six years old. There was a great party when a boy killed his first rabbit. Everyone ate some of the rabbit. But the boy could not eat any. If he did, the Penobscot believed the boy would never be lucky enough to kill a rabbit again.

In spring, Penobscot men often killed bears.

Penobscot hunters knew how to trick bears. When a bear saw a hunter, the bear stood up straight. It tried to hit the hunter with its front paws. The hunter threw a piece of wood at the bear. The bear always caught the wood. Then the hunter could get close to the bear. He could bring a stone ax down on the bear's head with a crash.

The men cut off the bear's head and hung it up on a tree trunk. They hung up the heads of all the animals they killed. Penobscot hunters believed this was how the animals wanted their heads to be treated.

The men skinned the bears and deer they killed. They took the skins home with them. The women made bed covers of bearskin. They made shirts and skirts out of deerskin. They made leggings and moccasins, too. They made birchbark boxes and dishes. Penobscot women were always busy. But they found time to weed the family corn fields.

12
THE PENOBSCOT
BY THE SEA

After their corn was picked in July, Penobscot families left home again. They paddled down the river to the rocky sea coast. They made camp on the beach. The children swam. But the children could not play all day. Even in summer, the Penobscot had to work hard for their food.

The men fished, or killed seals. The children helped their mothers catch lobsters and crabs and clams. Once in a while, the Penobscot had a special sea-food feast.

The Penobscot cooked clams and lobsters and crabs over a fire on the sand. Everyone ate and ate. Then the Penobscot carefully put all the shells back into the sea. They did this for a reason.

Like many Indians, the Penobscot believed fish were magic people. At times the magic people changed into animals or fish. Then they let themselves be caught so the Indians would have food to eat.

Most Indians believed the magic people would turn into animals or fish again and again. But only if Indians treated them well. To treat them well, the Penobscot put fish bones and shells back in the sea.

This is why they hung up the heads of the animals they killed, too. This is also why the Makah harpooner sang to the whales and gave them pretty feathers. Indians felt if they did not do these things, the magic people would grow angry. Then they would stop turning into food for the Indians to eat.

The Penobscot could not live if there were no animals or fish. In summer, they fished. In the fall, they hunted for moose. In winter, they hunted deer and elk. The Penobscot were almost always on the move, looking for their hard-won food.

13
MEET THE
MANDAN INDIANS

Many Indian tribes once lived near a part of the United States called the Great Plains. The Plains stretch from Canada down to Texas. The Plains are farmland today. But when Columbus discovered America, the Plains were grasslands. Vast herds of buffalo grazed on this grassy land in summer.

The Mandan Indians of North Dakota sent men onto the Plains to watch for these herds. So did the Pawnee of Nebraska, the Wichita of Kansas and the Caddo of Texas.

As soon as these scouts found a herd they ran back to their villages. They called out to their villagers that buffalo were near by!

In the Mandan villages, the men ran to their big, round houses. They got their bows and arrows. The women put corn and beans and squash into deerskin bags. Everyone hurried to get ready for the most dangerous hunt of the year. The buffalo hunt! To hunt buffalo, the Mandan had to go out on the Plains. There everyone had to sleep in very small tepees.

Mandan dogs could not pull the big poles needed to make big tepees. The Mandan used dogs to carry things. They had no horses. There were no horses in all America when Columbus arrived.

14
THE MANDAN
BUFFALO HUNT

The Mandan used a trap to kill the huge buffalo. They made their trap with clumps of stones. The two sides of the trap were far apart at one end. But the opening between the sides got narrower and narrower. The sides ended up very close together. They ended up at the very edge of a cliff.

The Mandan took blankets and hid behind the big stones. Everyone had to hide while the buffalo caller worked.

The Mandan believed it took magic power to trap buffalo. They believed their caller had this magic power. They believed only the caller could get the dangerous buffalo into a trap without frightening them.

A frightened buffalo herd always stampeded. A stampeding herd would knock over anything in its way. The Mandan could not get away from a stampeding herd. They could not run as fast as buffalo. If the buffalo stampeded before they were trapped, all the Mandan might be killed. So the Mandan were very quiet until the buffalo were in the trap. No one but the buffalo caller made a sound.

The caller wore a buffalo skin over his head and back. He moved very slowly. He crept close to the feeding herd. He swayed from side to side, the way buffalo do. Then he began to moan like a sick baby buffalo. The herd came toward him. The caller slowly moved toward the trap. The herd began to follow him. Little by little, the caller led the herd to the wide end of the trap. He led the herd all the way into the trap.

Then for the first time the caller moved fast. He ran out of the trap. The Mandan jumped up from their hiding places. Now they wanted to frighten the buffalo.

The Mandan waved their blankets.
They shouted.

The frightened buffalo started to
run. Then they stampeded. They
raced along the Mandan trap. They
came to the very edge of the cliff.

They could not stop. They went
headlong over the cliff.

Hundreds of buffalo fell to their death at the bottom of the cliff.

The Mandan had to be sure the buffalo were dead. A wounded buffalo was still very dangerous.

The Mandan stood at the top of the cliff and shot arrows at the buffalo down below.

The Mandan killed more buffalo than they could eat. They could not help it. It was very dangerous to try to kill buffalo one by one.

Mandan men skinned the dead buffalo. Then they cooked and ate all the buffalo steak they could hold. There was still a great deal left. The Mandan dried out as much of this meat as they could over smoking fires. The women and girls hung the meat on high racks. Then the dogs could not get it.

The women put the dried meat in deerskin bags. They tied the bags onto their dogs. They packed up the buffalo horns and bones, too. Then everyone started for home.

On the way, the Mandan often met other Indians who had been hunting buffalo. Indians who lived near the Plains did not all speak the same language. But they could all talk to each other. They "talked" by making signs with their hands and arms. Plains Indians could have long talks with each other without saying a word.

The Mandan were always glad to get home. Many families and all their dogs lived together in each Mandan house. There was just one big room in a Mandan house. Each family had its own bed next to the wall. The women cooked inside their houses.

The women cooked in clay bowls over one big fire. They cooked corn and beans and squash.

In the summer, Mandan men and women liked to work sitting up on top of their big, round houses. The women made new blankets and moccasins of buffalo skin. They used some of the skins to make new tepee covers. They would need them for the next buffalo hunt.

The men made spoons and cups of buffalo horn and bones. They used some of the buffalo skins to make round boats. When it rained, the men put a boat over the smoke hole in the house roof. Then the rain could not get into the house.

The men also used their round boats when they hunted bear and deer. They used them to cross rivers. It must have been hard to keep round boats from going in circles. But the Mandan managed.

15
THE INDIANS MEET
THE WHITE MEN

The Indians in America managed to do many remarkable things. They built houses though they had no nails. They cut down trees though they had no saws. They talked to one another though they did not all speak the same language.

Indians made boats to travel on rivers. They found ways to get over mountains. Hundreds of years later, wide roads would be built over many of the trails Indians once used.

Wandering Indian tribes probably learned many things from each other. Indians also learned new things every time they moved into a new part of the country.

Hunters who found no animals to kill learned to grow food. Others learned to catch fish.

The 2,000 Indian tribes in the United States were different from one another in many ways. Each Indian tribe had its own way of life.

Each tribe had its own laws and leaders. Each tribe had its own songs and dances. Each tribe had its own way of worshiping the gods it believed in.

Yet most tribes on the Northwest Coast were fishermen, like the Makah. Most of the tribes in the Southwest were farmers, like the Hopi. Indians along the Plains all hunted buffalo, like the Mandan. Other tribes farmed and hunted in the woods of the Northeast, like the Penobscot.

When the white man came, the America of the Indians changed. The white man brought horses with him to America.

In time, white settlers spread out all over the country. They began to build farms and towns and cities. They began to build a new America.

With the white man's coming, life became very different for the tribes whose forefathers had discovered America more than 20,000 years before Columbus was born. But that is another story.

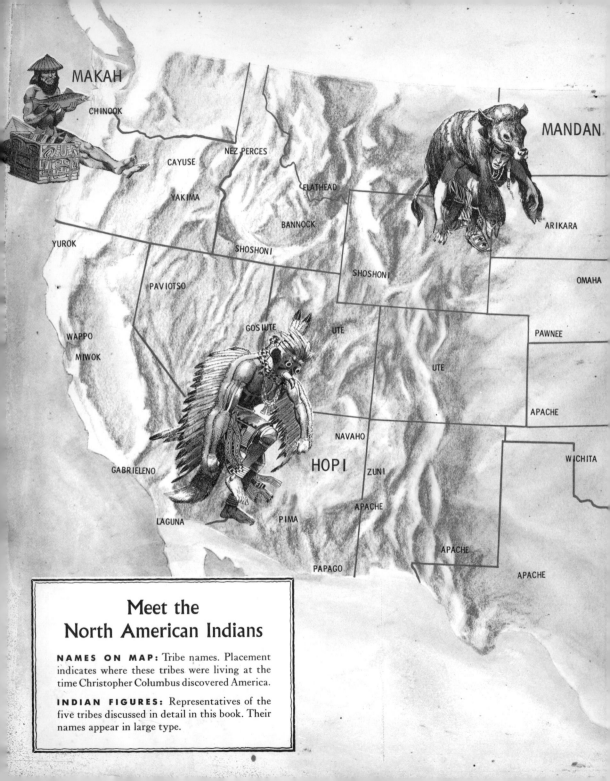

MAKAH

CHINOOK

MANDAN

NEZ PERCES

CAYUSE

YAKIMA

FLATHEAD

ARIKARA

BANNOCK

YUROK

SHOSHONI

SHOSHONI

OMAHA

PAVIOTSO

PAWNEE

WAPPO

GOSIUTE

UTE

MIWOK

UTE

GABRIELENO

HOPI

NAVAHO

WICHITA

ZUNI

APACHE

LAGUNA

PIMA

APACHE

PAPAGO

APACHE

APACHE

Meet the
North American Indians

NAMES ON MAP: Tribe names. Placement indicates where these tribes were living at the time Christopher Columbus discovered America.

INDIAN FIGURES: Representatives of the five tribes discussed in detail in this book. Their names appear in large type.